W9-AAE-436

j912.01 WADE
Wade, Mary Dodson.
Map scales

SEP 0 5 2013

WITHDRAWN

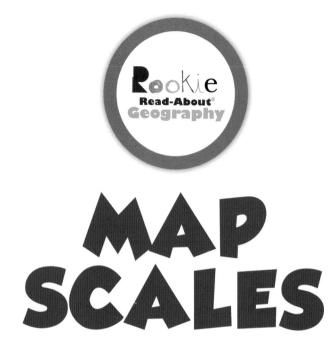

Rookie
Read-About®
Geography

MAP SCALES

by Mary Dodson Wade

Content Consultant
Laura McCormick
Cartographer
XNR Productions Inc.

Children's Press®
An Imprint of Scholastic Inc.
New York Toronto London Auckland Sydney
Mexico City New Delhi Hong Kong
Danbury, Connecticut

Library of Congress Cataloging-in-Publication Data
Wade, Mary Dodson.
  Map scales/by Mary Dodson Wade.
    p. cm.—(Rookie read-about geography)
  Includes bibliographical references and index.
  ISBN 978-0-531-28966-2 (lib. bdg.) — ISBN 978-0-531-29290-7 (pbk.)
  1. Map scales—Juvenile literature. I. Title.
  GA118.W35 2013
  912.01'48—dc23   2012003520

© 2013 by Scholastic Inc. All rights reserved.
Printed in China 62

SCHOLASTIC, CHILDREN'S PRESS, ROOKIE READ-ABOUT®, and associated logos
are trademarks and/or registered trademarks of Scholastic Inc.

1 2 3 4 5 6 7 8 9 10 R 22 21 20 19 18 17 16 15 14 13

Photographs © 2013: Getty Images/Antenna Audio, Inc.: 8, 24, 26; Media Bakery: 4
(Digital Art), 6 (Ronnie Kaufman), 28 (Tim Pannell); Shutterstock, Inc.: 22 foreground,
29 bottom left (Quang Ho), 10 (Rob Marmion).

Maps by XNR Productions, Inc.

Table of Contents

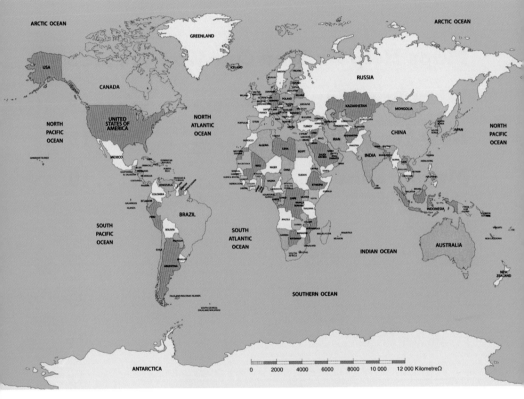

World Map

Maps Help Us Find Our Way

Maps are drawings of places.

Maps help guide us from place to place.

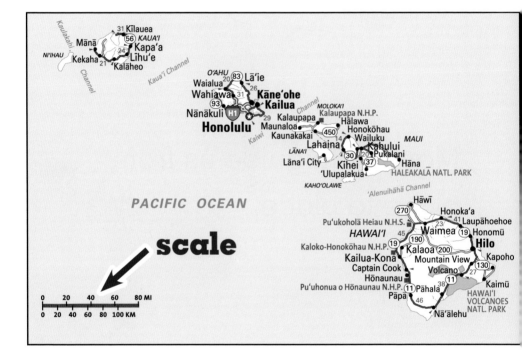

NI'IHAU

Kaulakahi Channel

Mānā
Kekaha 21
Kalāheo
Kapa'a
Līhu'e
31 Kīlauea
56 KAUA'I
24

Kaua'i Channel

PACIFIC OCEAN

scale

O'AHU
Waialua 20
Wahiawa 31
Nānākuli
Honolulu
La'ie 83
26 Kāne'ohe
Kailua
93
H1
29 Kalaupapa
Maunaloa
Kaunakakai

MOLOKA'I
Kalaupapa N.H.P.
Hālawa
Honokōhau
Wailuku
Kahului
Pukalani

Channel

Kaiwi

450
4
Lahaina
LĀNA'I
Lāna'i City
Kīhei
'Ulupalakua
30 20
37
Hāna

MAUI

HALEAKALĀ NATL. PARK

KAHO'OLAWE

'Alenuihāhā Channel

Hāwī
Honoka'a
270
23
41 Laupāhoehoe
Pu'ukoholā Heiau N.H.S.
HAWAI'I
45 Waimea
19 Honomū
Kaloko-Honokōhau N.H.P.
19 190
200
Hilo
Kalaoa
Kailua-Kona
Mountain View
Kapoho
Captain Cook
Volcano
130
Hōnaunau
27
Pu'uhonua o Hōnaunau N.H.P.
11 Pāhala 38
Kaimū
Pāpā
46
HAWAI'I
VOLCANOES
NATL. PARK
Nā'ālehu

0   20   40   60   80 MI
0 20 40 60 80 100 KM

8

What Is a Map Scale?

Sometimes we want to know how far apart places are. This is why maps have scales.

Scales help us measure the distance between places.

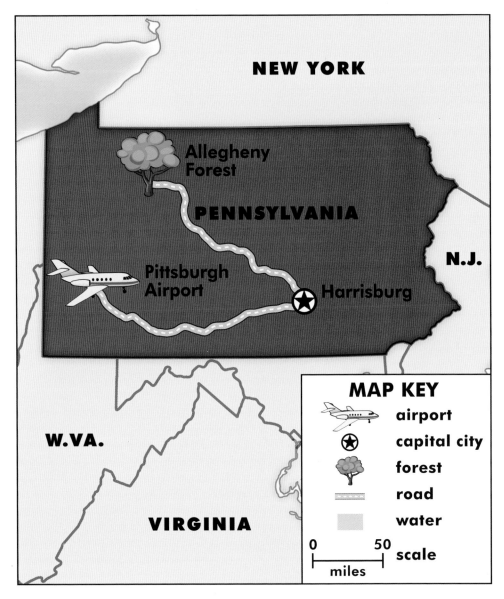

NEW YORK

Allegheny
Forest

PENNSYLVANIA

N.J.

Pittsburgh
Airport

Harrisburg

W.VA.

VIRGINIA

MAP KEY

airport

capital city

forest

road

water

0   50   scale
├─┼─┼─┼─┤
  miles

The scale can be shown on a line. Do you see the scale line on this map?

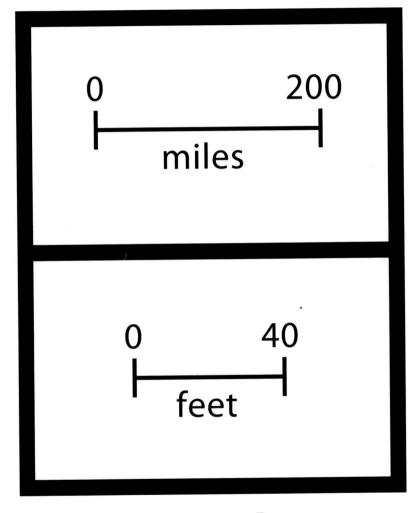

map scales

How Far Is It?

The scale has numbers.
They show what distance the
line stands for.

Look at this map scale. One inch stands for one mile.

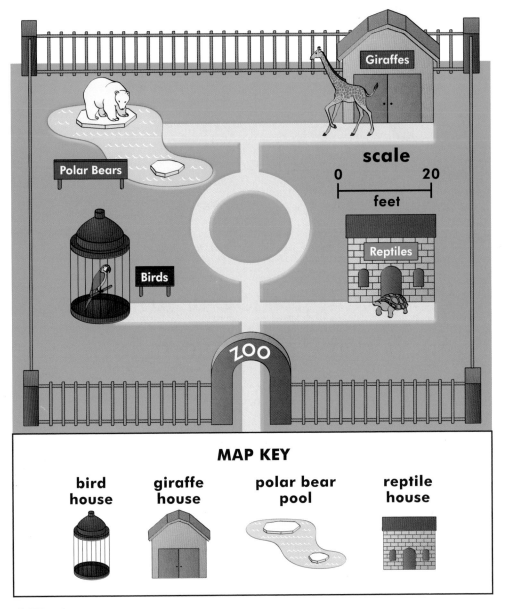

scale

0   20

feet

MAP KEY

| bird house | giraffe house | polar bear pool | reptile house |

Measure the Distance!

Some maps cover small spaces. This zoo map covers a small space. The scale stands for a short distance. One inch is the same as 20 feet.

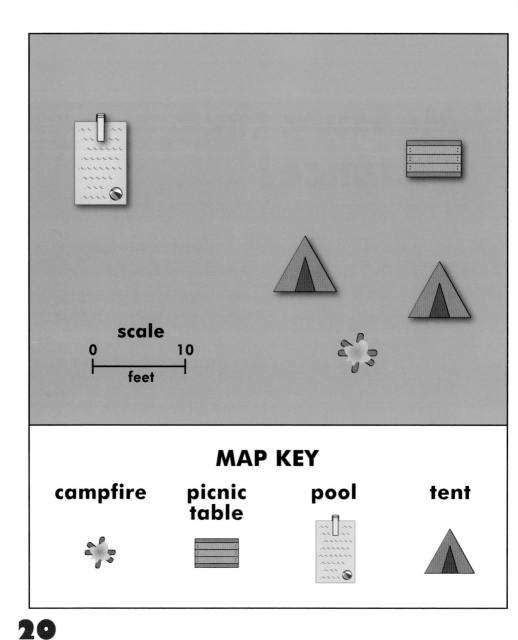

MAP KEY

campfire

picnic table

pool

tent

scale

0   10

feet

20

Look at this campground map. One inch is the same as 10 feet.

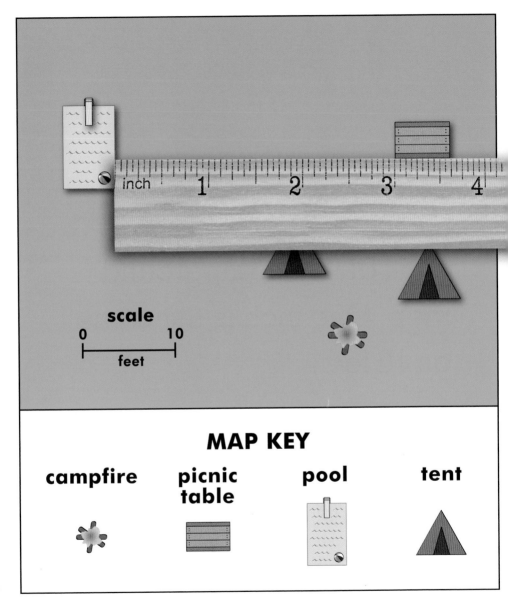

scale

0   10

feet

MAP KEY

campfire

picnic table

pool

tent

Use a ruler to measure the distance. The pool is 30 feet from the picnic table.

The United States

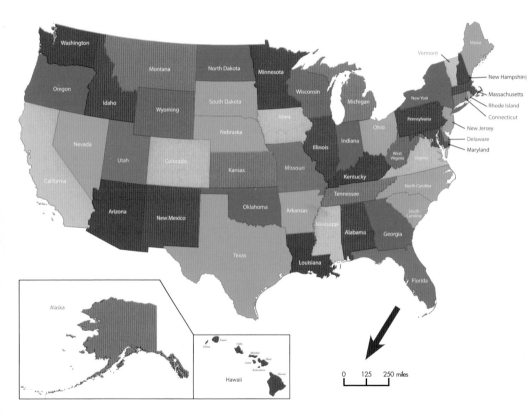

Washington
Montana
North Dakota
Minnesota
Oregon
Idaho
Wyoming
South Dakota
Wisconsin
Michigan
Vermont
Maine
New Hampshire
Massachusetts
Rhode Island
Connecticut
New York
Pennsylvania
New Jersey
Delaware
Maryland
Nevada
Utah
Colorado
Nebraska
Iowa
Illinois
Indiana
Ohio
West Virginia
Virginia
California
Kansas
Missouri
Kentucky
North Carolina
Arizona
New Mexico
Oklahoma
Arkansas
Tennessee
South Carolina
Mississippi
Alabama
Georgia
Texas
Louisiana
Florida

Alaska

Niihau
Kauai
Oahu
Molokai
Lanai
Maui
Kahoolawe
Hawaii
Hawaii

0   125   250 miles

Some maps cover big spaces. The scale stands for a big distance. Look at this scale. Colorado is about 250 miles from Nevada.

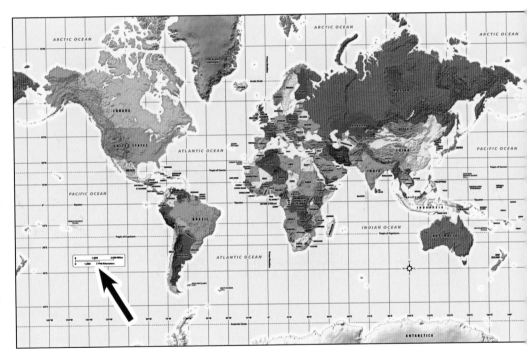

26

A world map covers a very big distance. This scale measures 2,000 miles.

Look at a map next time you go somewhere. How far will you travel? A map scale can show you the distance!

Words You Know

map

number

ruler

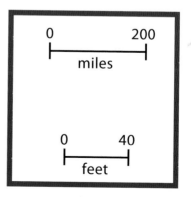

scale

TRY IT!

This is a map of a town. Look at the map scale. How far is the park from the school? How far is the airport from the school? You can use a ruler to measure the distance.

Visit this Scholastic Web site for
more information on map scales:
www.factsfornow.scholastic.com
Enter the keywords **Map Scales**

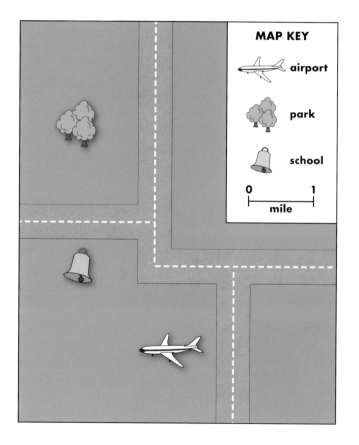

MAP KEY

airport

park

school

0   1
mile

Index

About the Author

Mary Dodson Wade spent 25 years helping children find books in the library, and now she writes books for them. She uses maps when she travels. She has petted llamas in Peru, watched elephants in Thailand, ridden a camel in Egypt, and seen pandas in China.